# THE HOLLOW LOG LOUNGE

# The Hollow Log Lounge

## Poems by R. T. Smith

UNIVERSITY OF ILLINOIS PRESS

URBANA AND CHICAGO

© 2003 by R. T. Smith
All rights reserved
Manufactured in the United States of America
1 2 3 4 5 C P 5 4 3 2 1

∞ This book is printed on acid-free paper.

Library of Congress Cataloging-in-Publication Data
Smith, R. T.
The Hollow Log Lounge : poems / by R. T. Smith.
p.   cm.
ISBN 0-252-02862-7 (cloth : alk. paper)
ISBN 0-252-07137-9 (paper : alk. paper)
I. Title.
PS3569.M537914H65      2003
811'.54—dc21      2002155078

# ACKNOWLEDGMENTS

Grateful acknowledgment is made to the editors of the following journals in which versions of many of these poems appeared over the past two decades: *Boulevard, Cold Mountain Review, Cotton Boll, Crab Orchard Review, Crucible, Cumberland Poetry Review, The Hollins Critic, Lonzie's Fried Chicken, New North Carolina Poetry, The Oxford American, Pembroke Magazine, Poem, Poetry Northwest, Prairie Schooner, Quarterly West, The Southern Review, Sundog,* and *Texas Review.*

I would also like to thank Brendan Galvin, Ron Coulthard, the late Oxford Stroud, Michael Combs, Stephen Gresham, Robert Overstreet, James Whitehead, Sam Buckhannon, Charles Frazier, Sharon Berman, Greg Hooven, Larry Lieberman, and, as always, my wife, Sarah Kennedy, without whose assistance and steady encouragement this book would never have been completed.

Further thanks are due the Virginia Commission for the Arts, Washington and Lee University, Annaghmakerrig, the Tyrone Guthrie Centre, and Poetry Daily.

*To the memory of John Hartford*

# CONTENTS

# THE HOLLOW LOG LOUNGE

# One Man's Sanctuary in Opelika, Alabama

Names count, and some buck called this hideout
the Hollow Log after its den dark and a stuffed
fox snarling over the bar. I park on a stool to kill
surplus brain cells and fuzzle my memory with spirits.
I study sweet Miss Pattie in her fishnet tights,
watch folks frisk by neon light to slow down the dying
or guarantee they'll live to see one more dawn as bright
as the drummer's jumbo cymbal. We live off the lean
of the land and keep the wolf from the door. Signs
at the state line declare *We dare defend our rights*,
but we really live by *Dixie, Roll, Tide*, or *War Eagle*,
and when the jukebox twangles out the lead-in
to "Stars Fell on Alabama," I commence to feel
neighborly enough to cross the dance floor and invite
the lady with curls red as vixen fur and a local grin
to help me shake off alimony and bills long overdue.
I'm already stepping lightly, all confident and male,
rolling sleeves past my heart and eagle tattoos.
I'll have one more before they shut off the lights.
My name is Sam Buckhannon. This is no fairy tale.
It's all fantastic and bizarre and true. It's my life,
a raspy song that sounds better if you sing along.

## Confession in a Booth at the
## Hollow Log Lounge


I seam towels for Dundee over in Georgia,
a non-union sweatshop with a dozen
rows of them blue glass windows all around.
Some of 'em says it's like a church.
Been there fourteen years, since just before
me and Hubert said vows at Devotee Baptist.
We've been divorced since eighty-four.
Seems he had another woman on the side.
Yessir, I been cold and warmed my hands
at the motor of my jury-rigged machine,
been Florida-hot and deaf from the fans
that don't do a damn bit of earthly good,
for me at least. I'm right fleshy, as you
can see. Been so hot I'd get the hives
and swell up like sourdough rising, but
I hardly miss a sick day, you understand.
I hate the feel when another woman's
been sewing on my machine. Substitutes
will break a needle or jack the floating
bobbin out of line. They don't give a hoot.
It ain't like they got a steady station
or reputation to uphold. This working's
almost a moral thing, Preacher Wilkes
would say, like marriage, and every thread
has got to be caught in the hem's edge
so the whole towel won't ravel first time
some salesman in a motel or shoe clerk

in his own home after a sweaty day
dries off from a cold shower bath. You see,
I know it don't take no giant brain
to sit behind a Singer machine and stitch
hour after hour, but I'm proud just the same.
I'm regular as a clock, and I don't dare fiddle
with another worker's machine. Some nights
I lie in my bed, once was my mother's,
and watch the gas flame jump beautiful blue
as the mill's windows and wonder how many
skins have been wiped dry on my towels,
and whose. It gives me a blushy pride
right on the edge of sleep. I'm over here
tonight with my sister Lily and her husband,
Buddy, supposed to be having a fine time
instead of talking my whole life at you.
This country and western band, specially
the drummer in a blue silk shirt, makes me
want to eat a hot pig's foot, drink beer,
and shake my tail. Let's show 'em a thing
or two. You ain't married just now, are you?

## A Local Doc, over Rocky Lunchtime Bourbon, Speaks of Barter and Hopeful Home Remedies

Nostrums? Lordy, I have seen them all.
Alcohol's the favorite. Many a quack's
panacea bottled in a cellar and hawked
from door to door is thriving still.

Bindweed's supposed to heal a bruise.
Cherokee remedies still survive,
and slave recipes—hyssop, juniper, chives.
Waitress, freshen this elixir, if you please.

One day a hefty woman who works a loom
down at Pepperell Mills sauntered in
with no appointment and perched herself prim
as an English queen in the waiting room.

What happened next? For a prolapsed
uterus, folk medicine recommends
inserting an Irish potato. It works,
if you can stand the weight, my friends.

Well, she'd relied on that specific
since winter. We'd hit, you understand, July,
and her complaint, not one bit shy,
was, *Leaves in my virginia.* Not beatific,

no, but she was composed, no maniac,
and it made some sense. What better place
than a protected pocket, warm and moist?
But the spud had sprouted, sent runners amok.

You never know in these flatland burley
counties if your manual skills will bloom
as sawbones or private gardener. Deftly,
I removed the obstruction and took it home.

I've raised a whole colony in my window box,
and bake, fry, or boil, I'm proud as hell
of this year's crop. The woman paid her bill
with eggs and applejack. Life is a paradox.

Now I've got to rush back and tend my flock.
Got appointments at four—a pregnant lady,
a leg to set, twins to inspect for chicken pox,
and Marvin with his routine emergency.

I guess you could say my practice is thriving.
Drop by, and I'll fry you up some shallot
hash browns in Margie's seasoned skillet,
a flavor I can promise is sure to revive

any ailing soul. Where do I get my onions?
Don't ask. The whole sweet world is a garden.

## Charlene Sperry on Safe Beauty

What I imbibe is a Virgin Mary—
tomato juice, Tabasco, and a stalk of celery.
No vodka, so I can watch the world clearly.

From what I see, this life is bloody
and dirty enough without whiskey,
which is alcohol and might explode.

And dancing's as bad. You breathe deep
and sweat like when you're angry
or in lust. It makes you look cheap,

except the waltz and Texas two-step,
where you touch, but just barely.
Mostly hands. I won't paint my lips

or let my skirt slip above my knees.
No smoking, pool shooting, or dirty
words. That pink in my cheeks is me,

not rouge, and undyed hair is my glory.
It's no sin to be pert, but nothing coy
or skimpy or too tight. Don't worry,

I'm not the type to judge others harshly.
That would be a sorry twist. I testify
for Jesus when I get a fellow eye-to-eye.

Like now. You know, it's a tragedy
how even upright folks will sully
the precious gifts of the Lord—modesty

not the least. If they studied scripture
they'd know about the coming Rapture
and what the hungry Devil has in mind.

I've got six friends who agree exactly.
We get together every Tuesday
and call our little clique Safe Beauty.

It's our Born Again self-defense,
but we also learned Christian karate
to keep our bones from harm. Good sense

tells us death happens. There's no drink
can change it. It was peach brandy
in fifths taught me that. Now I want to free

everybody from the pain. What do you think
evil is if not the lack of sympathy?
Your patrons—getting down or high or randy—

need to sober up and quit this tomfoolery.
Lord, can't these poor benighted people see
the world is an emergency?

## Flat-footing on Bluegrass Night: Dorsey Hostetter Explains It All to a Stranger

Banjo picks flash silver
as twilight on fast water,
and a Goshen oldster steps out
and drifts to the dance floor's
center. Born kicking
in the Blue Ridge to hard luck
and hardscrabble, he can still rise
limber in the spell of a fiddle.

Pivot and crossover, he bucks
the wing, his body stiff
but feet in time with "Sugar
Hill," as his friends step back
to let him shine. His trouser
pleats are sharp as hoe steel,
but he is clogging deep in bliss,
hot licks and hotter rosin,

as he follows Greg Hooven
bowing a freight train
straight from heaven,
and a solo whippoorwill
outside in the treeline
adds his three-note trill
to the dobro's drone. Hold still,
then join in the dance,

for what on earth, after all,
is beauty if not this moving
fast while nearly holding
still? Now click your heels
and get frisky. Footwork's
the best gift we have to offer
mountain children, pass it on
along with "Cherokee Rose"

and "Cold Jordan"'s moan,
which leaves us tapping toes
and hoping hard as we go down
the dark road winding home.

*He Gets Nostalgic in the Hollow Log Lounge*
*Just Before Friday Night's Last Call*

There's talk from locals that a girl can prove
her virtue by tying a cherry stem in two
with her unassisted tongue. My last love

could do it with ease, if gin's bitter shot
tamed the cherry's sweet taste to tart, but
she proved to be untrue, and I'm a lowdown sot

if it didn't cut me deep in the gut
when she left with a peg-legged guitar man.
She could shimmy, shiver, shake, and strut,

and I miss her a bunch. The way this band
plays "Let's Go Juking" brings her fancy dance
moves to my mind, and I say cherries be damned

and all other tests of eternal romance.
I'd shovel rock salt at the pickle plant
on graveyard shift to fandango in her trance.

## Pick It, Squirrel:
## Steve Gresham Sees the Light

Under the flashing stage lights six men
from far upriver strum the stand-up bass,
the git-box, banjo, fiddle. "Uncle Pen,"
"Fox on the Run"—a solo, a riff, a blend,
bottle glass sliding across a Gibson's neck,
until all eyes light on a scarecrow picker
in tight Levis and a burgundy shirt,
his white hair brushed to a rooster's shock.
He is beautifully strangling a mandolin,
but is he mouthing a grimace or a grin?
Short, and old as Elvis would have been, skin
strawberry, eyes jaybird blue, teeth bucked.
Oh, how can mortal fingers fly so quick?
As a drunk disciple shouts, "Pick it, Squirrel,"
I yearn to see such savage vision. Squirrel,
what secret do you see tuning this world
narrowed by your squint? You can lead us
beside still waters, fret the Devil's dream,
splitting the air with your wild discipline.
Not even the fiddler can play this nimble.
You've got the fire and down-home sizzle
in service to life swirled in live-wire frenzy,
saying praise must outshine the ordinary,
as if being on the trail to bliss were easy.
Give us an old-time run to burn out sin.
Tickle those strings till we shiver and spin.
Deliver us from evil. Beseech and bewail.
Pick it now, Squirrel, you blessed man.

## Theology in the Hollow Log

Missing Link my ass! You're Baptist as me
and too smart a man to believe *Argosy Magazine,*
no matter what you saw at the Village Mall.
No, I don't care if it is just a quarter.
It's fake, and I wouldn't go if you paid me.
Listen, all that monkey business is just one more
thing the college people have thought up
to make us believe they know something.
And another thing: you've been through silver
turnstyles before at a circus or movie. Turnstyle
is the sure sign of a fake. Okay, so the ice was real.
I got ice in my bourbon right now, but that don't mean
it come from the Bering Sea. I mean, if what you seen
was really a science find, why would it be on the road
taking quarters at shopping centers? Why they'd thaw
it out up there at John Hotkin College and find out.
They got tests, you know. It ain't like the lady
in gypsy getup guessing ages and weight at the fair.
Harry, Adam and Eve was people, like you and me.
Wadn't no Cheetah chimp in Eden. The real snakes,
though, is folks won't let your kids pray in school
to get right with Jesus and save their souls.
Them doctors at the college who say God is dead.
And you can always find some lost fool
with a scheme to fall in with 'em. Somebody says
one night at a party, "Let's make a dummy
of a hairy man and freeze it. Take it round and say,

'This is the Missing Link.'" And that *Argosy Magazine*'s
as bad for lies as the *National Enquirer*. Damn!
They just want you to doubt the Bible and bring
your family and loose change to see the thing.
Sure, I believe they got a thermometer to prove
just how cold they keep it. But can't nobody tell
for sure what's under there. And even if it is a body,
where it's missing from might be some trailer park
down in Florida or a Boy Scout camp in Vermont.
Them con folks'll stop at nothing. Here, have a drink
and forget what you seen. Next week they'll be
trying to ram a snake show down our throats or
getting a rock band in front of J. C. Penney
to drive everybody into the store. Them folks
at the shopping center don't believe it either,
but they think you might buy a pair of shoes
or orangeade while you're there. If you know
what's good for you, you'll just drink up
and listen to what Preacher Wilkes has to say
about false idols. Okay, I don't give a hitch what
you do, but let me alone and don't talk about it
again. Like pro wrestling. Watch it and have fun,
but don't fall for all that cheapshot pretend.
Yeah, you can go back till your paycheck's shot
for all I care. There wasn't no monkeys in Paradise.
Harry, you drink too much or not enough.
And quit gaping jungle-eyed into your ice.

## Wade Seego Believes
## Soylent Green Is People

Down here we say we dare defend our rights,
our state motto. I'd back Charlton Heston
for any office in the land. A Christian,
he speaks right up. He's got his head on straight,
and people listen. Even on the screen
of a honky-tonk TV he still looks
like a hero, and he wouldn't let freaks
take over our country. If it takes firepower
to keep us free, I say stock up. Keep your
powder dry. Everything is dangerous
these days. Life sucks. We suck too. Disaster
is coming. Even God's gone spleenish. Bless
the common man against the government.
They lie. They grind us up. Winchesters
might be our last resort. Hellfire preachers
say we best prepare for a dark event,
but maybe Charlie Heston could keep death
off our backs and tone down Jehovah's wrath.
Sweet Jesus—and this is the gospel truth—
is pissed off at our newfangled unfaith.
He's coming back, and he's armed to the teeth.

## A Cosmological Discovery in the Hollow Log Lounge

She'd been a cosmetologist, she confessed,
for two decades, as I paid for her first
green piña colada and made my request:
"Tell me something of the cosmos, lady,"
as Patsy Cline yodeled on the Wurlitzer
jukebox. Winking, she inhaled a Swisher
Sweet and passed my philosophy test.

"Most folks believe they'd be mighty pretty,"
she said, sipping her cool coconut elixir,
"and reckon the right hairdo and lip liner
would show the world's there's boocoo beauty
hiding inside." She smiled like new money
and bit her candied cherry in two,
said, "Darling," she said, "it ain't true."

## Tull Jackson's Slow Confession

"Just because God fed those saints in the wilderness
doesn't mean He's going to keep His eye on us,
unless we find ways to make Him hear our voice."

So says my wife, and she's always got a scheme.
Last month: a chain letter guaranteed to redeem
any pious soul who believes in the Supreme

Being and sends every name on the list a dollar.
I used to dismiss her foolishness as glandular,
female time-of-life stuff. I said, "Try Mars bars

or something else with chocolate." Now she keeps
her desperations secret. Or tries. Just this week
a package arrived. Thinking I was deep asleep,

she opened it in the pantry, but I sneaked up
and spied. She was kneeling, wearing a showercap
with an evangelist's palm print on the top,

an ink outline where Jonah'd blessed the plastic.
It made me sad to see my own wife turned tragic.
She used to teach middle school arithmetic

and had a glowing smile no human could resist,
but after Jim Beam convinced me to give up Christ
for riverside honky-tonks, the Methodist

in her fell sadly awry. A man's heart will freeze
one way, woman's another. After that, reprieve's
unlikely. If I could raise a prayer, I'd say, "Please

grant the woman blissful peace. She's not to blame."
She can't carry children. Some fluid in her womb
is wrong. She believes it's her fault just the same.

Her kind needs to be blessed almost as bad as mine
needs to imbibe and feel regret and suffer shame.
I wish the mercy God would earn His golden name.

Something starving in my heart is set to scream.

## In Horsehide Shoes, Fleur Hobbs Eats Cheese, Drinks Irish Beer, and Laments the Nature of Her One Arrest

I see so much potato love—Steve Killough's
term—where people fear slow solitude
and bond with any friendly foe who's good
for a hungry touch. A bad quid pro quo,

if you ask me, when the soul craves wildfires
that purify—call that love passion fruit.
To settle for less is cynical. I root
for risk, but my history's this: one prior

arrest for crossing Oxford Street, lost and drunk.
A night in jail with my best gal friend, hugging
the bars and humming "Swing Low," thirst slaked

and worry rising fast. If you go hunt
a rap sheet more dull, you'll lose. Just hanging
from a public oak would improve it. I ache

to be caught upside down, a keepsake
on a bough, singing, swinging, buck naked
with another human and possum grinning,

but Daddy Ed would likely pay the fine.
He's always there to get me off the hook.
I'm just a potato. My spunk is fake.

Pour me another Harp. I want life spinning.

*Break Time: Herman Wiggins Just About Says*
*It All to a Fledgling Who Hopes Swing Music*
*Turns the Local Girls to Carnal Dreams*


Don't talk easy women, son, to a man
who's at peace behind a Fender pedal
steel. Have a cool Coors and set a spell
in this dismal bar. Hell, it ain't no shame

to be alone. Twice divorced, now I aim
to please the crowd, fingerpicks and thimble
singing on sweet strings. I use the biblical
method: *Seek and ye shall find,* a plan

the lonely and trouble-prone endure. You see,
boy, some truth's not in the *Broadman Hymnal:*
homemade know-how says bright rainbows
don't follow every storm, so I avoid wild gals.

Better to marry or burn? The Devil
can take me before another Jezebel.
"I've got all I need to drive me crazy,"
according to the gospel straight from Mel

Tillis, and I know you know he knows.

*Getting Cleared: The Cosmetologist*
*Recounts Her Recent High-Noon Ordeal*


Mystic Barbie swans in here Wednesday,
her velvety skirts aswirl, patchouli
stink all over her like white on rice.
She wants Euroblack to revive her raven

locks and make her look under forty.
In mid-fantasy she stops to testify
to her hard past, which has turned her obsessed
with Dianetics, becoming a "cleared."

What she says—it was just yesterday—
is that L. Ron Hubbard, whose Scientology
is a business religion, proved aliens
diseased our spirits. Her coffee shop coven

ponders it all morning. She never works,
and the grapevine says not even sex
talk can distract her homemade intellect
from "reactive thinking" and "psychic locks,"

stuff leaking from the past to hold her back.
You know, *Issues.* She calls herself "Francine,"
but her real name's Frances. The get-rich-quick
gurus say you catch more flies with fancy,

so she traded up. She told me this:
you know how pious folks can sometimes find
the features of Jesus or even Elvis
in clouds or ground beef or a dying pine?

Monday she and her auditor—that's what
Scientology dupes call their confessors—
had been untangling hang-ups. They were
hoping to limit her snits and temper.

Wore out, she napped, then woke up and went
to fetch some wine from the cabinet.
There, in maple grain, sure as a crow shines black,
she saw her own face staring back, eyes dark

as wet coal, thinning hair turned thick as thatch.
"I had a halo," she said, "angelic
as anything you'll ever see in church."
She hadn't been so worked up, that bitch,

since Nazi Ollie North shook her pasty hand.
She felt her spirit washed and split ends gone.
Presto! Her sins forgiven, the road
to bliss in sight. She told me I should join

and expose my past lives. I could get cleared,
then get rich helping her enlist others. My
ambitions were smaller. I rinsed her dye
into the sink and let the blow-dryer

drown her babble. I'd had more than my share
of New Age, cosmic rays, and E-meters.
I didn't want anything else under the sun
but a salon clear of patchouli fumes,

a sane earthwoman under my scissors.
I wanted our village princess gone
back to her gossip and bottomless cup
at the no-count crackpot coffee shop.

I was already by-God clear about that.

## Cadmon Dabney from Whitby Corners on How He Made His Song

Around the poker circle at Hilda's house
I'd swig my Bud and fold, let the pot
fall to the friendly ring of local studs.

Wild card blind, double-down, or bluff,
my heart was never in the game.
I'd ante up and hear the common gossip,

but soon I knew they'd joke and sing
and tell amazing stories while I kept mum,
not ever having learned the art of idle talk.

They'd laugh and ask, "Cat got your tongue?"
It's the meek beasts I like, anyway, a Guernsey
steaming by her stool and ready to be milked,

doves nestled in, the dog, chickens snug
on their racks, lambs. I'd find myself a cause
and steal out to the barn where I kept

my autoharp in a box. Lying back on straw,
I'd strum the strings: "Working on the Railroad"
or "Worried Man." Those players had their

ways of praising life with wild red jacks,
and Heaven maybe liked the rising smoke
from Tampa Jewels and the way they'd break

into a tune. All I had was eight quick
fingers, a sheaf of strings, until one night
when a storm put out the lights. I was

playing for the animals when it went dark,
and in the shadows—I felt half asleep—
I saw my breath take on a shape.

It was weird and rising, a man so bright
I knew he hailed from another place,
and he said, "Sing, Cad, you're no mute.

Tell of the world you know's a marvel."
Then I was humming a tune I didn't even
know I knew. It wasn't about any king-

high straight nor heart flush. Pure praise
for what is, the shimmer on things
was the tune I called "New School Glory,"

and then I sang for the splendor, birds
of the air, deer gathered at the river. Jesus,
it was lovely, me and not me. The loft

shook bright as fire, only smokeless and cool.
I danced pure rapture for the universe,
chapter and verse, then everything went still

and hushed as the inside of a zipped-up Bible:
I saw His gold face flaming over the stalls.
He raised His arms like silver wings. I said,

"Yes, Lord, yes, I see your raise and call."

## Dew Stuart's Breakthrough on the Jew's Harp

Because any village blacksmith
could fashion one, they were common
as roadapples, even before the banjo
crossed the Atlantic in chains.

I've always wondered how it got
that name, since "juice harp"
and "jaw harp" make more sense.
It's sharp and tarnished and shaped

like the better mousetrap people crave.
One night I kept holding mine up
to moonlight, figuring different
grips. I never understood chords

and keys, pitch and harmony.
I'm glad it's just a lonesome drone
and more sprung bedspring than melody,
but my mother's father took it

seriously enough to forge a few,
the hot hammer clinking time
onto bent steel. He'd accompany
the Monroes or Acuff on the radio

while I shuffle-stepped and floated
across the parlor's bright pine.

Because I'd sworn not to quit
until I knew the secret, I leaned

on a cold oak that winter night
and turned it everywhichaway
against my mouth. I bit the flange
and sucked in starlit air. I blew

and tweaked the tongue, listening
to the way it trembled less musical
than wind in the boughs around me.
Sweetening the lesson with peach

schnapps, I wanted a song to flower
and speak across the icy river.
My hands were stiff with weather,
and just when I was ready

to surrender and attend to owls
prowling down in the valley,
I blundered into a tight clamp
with my lips that let me twang out

a couple of tunes to the audience
of stiff hemlocks, as if to prove
what's crucial for anything you desire:
you kiss it hard and soft at once,

give the breath a twist of the dark,
if you're desperate or homesick
and resolved at last to save yourself
with the least thing we call music.

## Oxford Stroud Recollects Fishing
## with Electricity

I've caught fish everwhichaway they can be.
On the Chattahoochee River I've used nets, gigs,
trot lines, and bare hands. Even electricity.
One day Braleigh and me caught so many
that two-ended punt boat nearly went under.
We were boys and didn't know any better.
Catfish were plentiful as water for all
we could figure. That was back then.
We'd wrap the copper pipe and drop it in,
then use the telephone battery to make a wet cell
of that whole muddy dogleg of the river.
The small channel cats would rise, then
recover, but big whites and blues would float,
belly up, and we'd haul 'em in, fill the boat
to the oarlocks with fresh fish to eat or sell.
Their backs shined so bright it was a wonder.
But let me tell you this: it was also a danger.
If you caught the coil wrong or touched iron
binding on that old craft with a live wire,
it was enough to knock you on your ass.
A man could get killed just trying to catch fish.
Of course, such a method was a sin against Jesus
and man, fish and fresh water, but we didn't savvy.
We were just free as gnats for the summer,
a little enterprising and a little hungry.
Besides, we hadn't heard of sport or mercy.
That was a cooter's age ago. That was then.

## The Phyllis

My husband was in the CIA. That's the kind
of woman I am. Lived all over Asia in suites
decked out for the embassy staff, lounged
around pools with sweet Singapore Slings,
but now that I'm on my own, I can't stand
to waste a minute, not a breath. You may know
my regular work at Helen's Mademoiselle
Beauty Nook downtown, but on the side
I help women trim their belly fat. "Lose
weight now, ask me how." A thin American
girl is a happy one, I always say. Oprah, too,
but the drugs witch doctors sell can kill
brain cells quicker than liquor. And your will,
your liver. Listen, herbs are just what
you need to cut that cellulite. I learned
that in the Orient. I had spare time to spare
and paid attention. Embrace herbs and exercise
daily with a proper purge, just like the monks
of Buddha. Tablets help, and fruit shakes, too,
make you frisky as a prime-time preacher,
but here's my recent love and pleasure:
invention. True, I mixed a chemical rinse
that made great colors like the *ao dais* in Saigon,
but some of the girls said it burned. Then
I worked with Gene Graddick on a special
quick perm you can get wet, but he cut out
before we got it perfectly perfected. Beauty,

though, that's the ticket. I knew that even in Nam,
while Jim-ass was off on his secret missions.
The new machine I'm the mother of will move
senior citizens and the, you know, "crippled"
gals to the swivel chair without a hitch. I saw
too many women, men, and sad children
with stiff legs (or one or none) who couldn't
move after one government or another gave
invitations to mortar fire or a claymore mine.
With this machine I could prop them straight
and wet-cut any willing guinea pig—pardon
my calling the handicapped that—blow dry
and comb them out with no inconvenience.
My prototype is getting made in a LaGrange
body shop this minute, if Bish is working
late like he promised, and I aim to franchise,
since Jim left me flat busted—well, you can
see that's a figure of speech—with back bills
piled to the ceiling. The government has laws
that business can't fairly slight the challenged,
so if I get it right, it's got to sell. I can't
tell you how it works, you know. I learned
secrecy from an expert, covert fool. It's called
"The Phyllis," after me.

                    What's wrong with that?
It's no brag if you really did it. Hell—excuse
my French—you know Snake Grillis of Snake
and the Grass? He can pick the fiddle better
than any man alive, and says so on stage.
It's no lie, so let him waller in it, I say. Look,
I'm salt of the earth and have all the right
attitudes and skills, not that selfish royal act
my Jim put on when we went to the market.

He called the people "slants" and laughed
when they didn't savvy. It's no wonder
he carried a Colt in his belt; they could tell
how superior he felt, and they hated him hard.
That asshole—pardon my French, but it's so.
         No thanks, I stick to coffee. Hard stuff
was what my ex used to wet his whistle
and make him sharp for following spies,
and cocaine, too, I suspect. Myself, I don't
need a jumpstart when loving's on my mind.
I got a tummy tuck, a boob job, a wardrobe
straight from Penney's Gay Parisian line.
You're a devil, but you smile like a G.I. on leave,
and I can cure your entire cowlick problem.
I've got a chair and a whole outfit at home,
plus a queen waterbed and a Sony VCR
on credit. I'm maxed out! Grab your jacket,
buckaroo, and to hell with any sour memories.
I've got bourbon and branch, black lace,
and oodles of time. I've got a Walther
in my purse and boudoir kung fu tricks for two.
I'm here now and just for you. Call me Phyllis
or *The* Phyllis or Boo, then just call me in time
for breakfast. Ain't this a lucky rendezvous?

## After One Straight Jack Too Many, the Salesman Waxes Wild

God bless Mr. Daniels's distillery!
See that gal in the translucent blouse?
If she steps between your eyes and the light,
you'll discover what sight was made for. Let's move
over. That big bar mirror doubles the world,
and two of me is more than I can stand.
That sombrero on the wall puts me in mind
of what folks will buy to make life worth more.
We live by what we see from day to day.
Last week I sold four sets of flamingos
out on Old Dowd Road. This year I find
the favorite color's fuchsia, a color
you wouldn't see in just any man's dream.
That waitress in the tight red jeans could show
you the wicked side of Heaven in the dark!
But what I mean is, folks dancing here are
desperate for action they can imagine while
taking a breath at work. Cocaine cowboys
and secretaries, housewives whose husbands
booked out, mechanics and all the rest. They sway
and down the magic drinks that make it all
like a picture show in tune with cheap
bands from across the river. Some will cross
the Chattahoochee just to gain an hour. Central
time is better, and anything east of here has
already happened. Hell, these people want

the same as me and you—surprise or fights,
or a kind word to get them through weeknights,
some color snapshot deep inside the mind.
See this checked shirt of go-light green?
Just last week it picked up a fine lady
whose paycheck comes from Goodyear Tire.
Took an hour after I took her home to explain
that I've got a steady in Montgomery.
She thought we were in some kind of movie.
You see, the shirt did all the work. Image
is the future, all we need to be happy. I sell
birdbaths and plastic geese to rural people
who want to fancy their yards. Strange taste
is what I bet on, count on mobile homes
with mimosa trees and few real flowers
to tell me where to call. I'm dizzy now
from watching battalions of sparkles flash
on the floor and ceiling. See that eight-point
buck who's stuck his head right through
the wall? That's how it looks, but Bobbie
Dilly Russ, the bartender's wife, shot him dead
on the edge of their garden plot. She was
too shocked to see him as yard decoration.
Besides, he was live. Speaking of the truly
living, let's see if the two blonde pixies would
care to dance to this last awesome tune.
And don't get me wrong. Purple birds
made of eternal plastic can have a beauty too.
They can't spread wings and fly, but they capture
your eye and say, "If the world is a squirrelly
circle spinning in space, this could be the center."

## Politics and Vodka in the Hollow Log Lounge

His Ignorance the Governor sits up in Montgomery
making proclamations and decrees in the name
of honesty and education while the sneaky money
rolls in at his plant—Universal Conceptions.
Don't that fancy name sound a right smart shady?
I used to bass fish his pond down Silver Hill way
at dawn, watch the herons rising from the shore,
bigmouth making rings across the water. I don't
usually approve of poaching, but his secret water
somehow seemed just right to be an exception.
They shovel in the profits, his thick-necked family,
from making machines to exercise your body.
The discount stores sell the things to fools
too slick and busy to heft feed sacks in the barn.
He played ball at 'Bama, so he knows that stuff.
Like most, he slipped through, missing classes,
but it sure galls the likes of me to have to see him
cutting capers on the TV for the whole damn
world to see and judge us by. Once he came on
with a rope tied on some papers, then said
how he aimed to harness the budget. Big laugh,
him wobbling on his hind legs, but hell's bells,
that man's forever shaving funds and quoting
scripture wrong, trying to strangle the whole state
in his "firm hands," the rolled-up sleeve approach,
the better to dig deeper in our pants pockets.

He swears he's a man of the people, and some
who believe more in moolah than democracy
go out of their way to follow. The rest—
we are a sorry bunch, the paranoid minority—
drink heavy. Now this one-horse Holiday
Inn is all worth celebrating from Huntsville
to Mobile. Me, I'm salting away some money
to move west, shuffle over to sad Mississippi
where times are raw and harder but more true.
They say a wealthy bully has no need to steal,
but power makes the rich so bold and filthy
they're not content without your soul. I'd be
moving on myself, if I was you. Not even free
fish are worth the horror here. Don't you smirk
at me like this is just a yellow-dog Democrat's
opinion. His promises about low taxes are bait
wiggling, hiding the sharp steel of a fool hook.

# Cowgirl

In Stetson and calico vest, spandex
and Calvin jeans, she was the best
at the bar. Does Gucci make range boots?
Hers were snakeskin with heels
like railroad spikes. The rest you could
guess: eyes the blue of West Texas yonder,
complexion like hot coffee with cream.
All night I gave her slack but kept
my dally-knot tight, hoping she'd like
the stories I could tell—drunk Indian
twins fighting with icepicks in Cheyenne,
Carolina moonshine, deer breaking open
watermelons out of crazy hunger.
Regular as breath she'd say, "Damn!" or
"Yes!" and stomp a heel through sawdust
to the pine floor. I nearly had the rest
of my life planned out, downing Coors
and forking out for God-knows-whose,
till a dude in a Brooks Brothers suit
moved in, flashing a wad of Andrew
Jacksons like cold cash grew on trees,
and she said to me—she fairly spat it—
"Get lost!" So I did, prostrate all night
in a roadside hay field, watching the sky
sleek as a coal-black stallion's flank.
Damn if every star wasn't a spur
burning its wheels into my foolish eyes.

## Zydeco Washboard, the Confession of Johnny Smooth

Momma behind the springhouse rubbing clothes
on tin ridges the color of catfish
might scrape her knuckles. The clouds of suds
running from the tub big as a bass drum
tinted pink. Peafowl in the peach tree screamed,
and wind shook the scarecrow's coat. I wonder
if she thought, feeling the steady shocks
in her shoulder bones, that scrub-board was rough
as the road past our house, the hard ride
on a pulpwood truck, ribs of a hungry child.
First time I saw a chanky-chank man
strum a washboard with his thimbles, I was
stunned to discover how labor might make music.
Soon I learned table spoons and the whangsaw
just needed clever hands and a will to stand
behind the fancywork of bosses with guitars.
Things that clink and racket set the rhythm
while the squeezebox pumps a Cajun strut.
Cowbell and pail, hammer on the sawblade's
bow, I can chase these chord boys deeper
into hot pepper and Jax than any coon-ass
fiddle plucker. Just thinking of my home roots
and raising a ruckus I learned behind the church,
I can rattle the beer taps till they bleed.
I can make every roadhouse sinner dance
like being scrubbed in a Zydeco stampede.

## A Putative Country Star Rebukes
## His Exit Escort

You has-been jock, I'll tell you this for free:
my voice is golden, platinum, honey.
I put this state on the map. I'll be as noisy

as I like. You'd know my name. The Devil
himself taught me "Hellhound on My Trail,"
you know, Robert Johnson's favorite wail.

Six-six-six, that's the strings on three guitars.
Don't mess with me. I'll buy this goddamn bar
and put you on the street. My red Telstar

cost more than your dream house. That customer
who said I was hassling his kid sister
ain't worth the river of shit you'll enter

if you don't take your mitts off my jacket.
That's Italian leather. And she wasn't
his sister any more than this cheap joint

is the Opry. I dropped in for a draught,
to hear the yokel talent for some laughs.
That redneck tried to collect my autograph

with money, then nasty words, then force.
When crazy fans like him get in my face,
I have to teach them it's safer to be nice.

It's the minstrel's habitual hazard:
we get this crap because the world is sad,
because suffering out loud calms the blood.

No thickwit bouncer can treat me like this.
Remember me next time you hear "Christmas
in Dixie." Yeah, I wrote that. Kiss my ass.

## Twang Chic: Sam Buckhannon
## Explores the Latest Fashion

If it's true that Johnny Weismuller stole his Tarzan yell
from the Alpine yodel, did Hank Williams in the back seat
of his Cadillac dream the ululation of Bedouin women

welcoming the horsemen back from war? When I was a boy
only a fool would fake a country sound, and my father
made his voice over to ring as simple as Jack Parr's

Midwest porkless, yamless, no-cornbread-or-cracklin' patter.
He didn't want to be from Butts County, Georgia, and hated
farm chores and coveralls. Football got him out. The FBI

gave him a way to travel under cover, but I have heard him,
years later, after choir practice and the church social,
sit back with a Pall Mall and follow Eight-Finger Fleming's

banjo frail. He'd hold that smoke deep, his ash glowing till
his throat was bathed in tar, and then he'd cut loose and scroll
it out, a yodel to make Roy Rogers blush. It was no hymn,

I'll tell you. We had a brick split-level in the suburbs,
and the radio station of choice adored Perry Como's croon.
My mother adopted words like *boocoo* and *oodles* to mask

her peach-orchard drawl. An uncle might tell a farmer's
daughter joke, the rake fleeing the cocked shotgun
stopping on a hill to yodel, "Andyouroldladytoo,"

but nobody could say *ain't* or *you'uns* or *I'll get to it
directly* without a sharp correction. Country music
was not Frank Proffitt or Dock Boggs, but rubes

like Porter and Loretta Lynn, backwoods fabrication
of waist jackets and swirl skirts, long nights on a bus
with Grapette and gin. "Hillbillies," the neighbors laughed,

and mother hated her mill-town roots so much she whispered
around a Tom Collins, "I'm half Jewish." But if she sipped
often enough, something would catch her funny bone

and you'd hear the accent clear. Everybody wanted
to ditch their chifforobes and pie safes, get matching sets
from Ethan Allen, eat ravioli and pave the drive. *Denial,*

experts would say, but the cracker backlash is now
upon us, every professor and Appalachian scholar
desperate to sound authentic, to drop the terminal

r and double the syllables, to say *bodacious* or *I favor
apple fruit* or *Would you kindly wallop my dodger?*
We want it nasal as the shiver of a juice harp's

tin tongue. We crave it riddled with mongrel grammar,
the sinus cavities set all a-tremble. We want to taste it
with sorghum syrup, to catch that yokel power,

desperation, the provenance of a Depression fiddle.
If a Swiss watch pops its mainspring, what echoes
is Hank's bourboned backstage nasal quaver

clearing a path for "Long Gone Lonesome Blues."
Call it hick bliss tinged with mimosa scent
and pig lots, Tuberose, greens. Say it's bumpkin

vogue or red clay homegrown slang: it holds my
Adam's apple in gawky thrall, and I still claim it,
the whole history of shaped pain shaved down

by local oafs and red-faced rustics—in short, us—
shackled in our Caliban stage to yawp and Celtic keen,
ravenous fashion's *dernier cri,* country slur,

twang chic sweeter than honey or money or—
running through the red clay gully—the forlorn
moan of the midnight Macon train.

# Country Music

This might be a myth, but I have to tell you
just the same. Praise Him. You heard
how Riddy Eury was snakebit

handling copperheads and canebrakes
at Ezra Church despite her husband begging
she quit the Holiness. He said come back

to solid-ground Baptist where don't nobody
shake and tonguespeak nor try
to charm the snakes with a glory quartet.

She got it on the wrist. Her arm swole
purple and her gospel people took her off
so the doctor called by her legal spouse

could not treat her till her heart burst. Praise
His name: that's all fact. And you know
her husband, O. R. Shupe, was a popular player,

giving folks whiteman sorrow, cotton boll
blues, full moon woe frailed out on his magic
mandolin. Well, he went into a grief

bluer than anything before, just wailing
and making up songs on the spot. He was out
at the Oasis, the Spur, and the Hollow Log

with ballads about how the Lord turns evil
in the mouths of Holiness preachers taking
the Bible for an easy truth or simple.

Say hallelujah. The Devil lurks somewhere
in this story. We need to set him running.
At the funeral O.R. cut the fool, leaped

into the grave, and tore at the coffin. He swore
he'd charm her back and picked that night
over the mound till his fingers bled.

I know some are saying maybe this couldn't
happen. Some of you are doubting,
but he heard her voice coming up

from the flowers. Then it was sirens,
and the sheriff took him off. Next day
he was downtown singing a demon's hymn

about how the Holiness people are killers,
how they love the God of death.
That's when a van of sisters stopped

and dragged him in, hauled him up
to the cliffs over where Copperhead Creek
feeds the Redrust River. They aimed

to throw a scare into his heart. The Holy
Ghost has stranger ways. O.R.
fell over the rim into a wire fence

that cut his head from the body. Praise
Jesus, a miracle came on, his voice
not stopping when his head rushed

through the narrows where water white
as a hawk's breast roared. Was this
his right anointing? His people claim

they'll build a marker with his name
and a mandolin carved in granite
and the words saying he loved a woman

more than the rest of the world. Some
call it blasphemy and say they'll not stand
for it. The Shupes claim they'll defend it

night and day, and they'll have rifles.

## One-Eye Remembers Silver Queen

For the glorious Fourth, normal sweet corn
was not enough. Alton shut the garage,
shoved Lily and me in the truck, and took
off toward the Gulf and "richer soil,
salt on the wind, even the tassel silks
worth chewing." Two hours, toward dusk,
radio gospel sparking with blue static,
Lily straddled the shift and leaned
on Alton's tattoo: *U.S. Army, Death
to Ruskies* and an *X* of swords. She kissed
his lobeless ear, his neck under the grease
that slicked his hair blue-black as Elvis.
Cheek to the breeze, I watched all south
Alabama smear by on pillar pines, shacks
weathered to old bone, kudzu hells
and fields of cotton, soy and corn. Cows.

At the roadside stand we could see shrimpers'
rigging beyond the roofs. The farmer
swore every kernel was a perfect pearl.
"I toss the shucks to my sows and stoats,
and they sing." I could hear a flicker's
bill chisel on a live oak, see the first
fireflies dazzle the marsh. The road back
north went faster, two headlights ensuring
every soul was safe. The radio crackled
and could not carry a tune on the eve

of simmering Independence Day. Lily's
hand crawled on his Levis, so I shut
my eyes to think of a spitted pig,
gallons of sweet tea and Silver Queen
slathered in butter. A Mobile station
gave us Sleepy LaBeef moaning over
his "Corinna, Corrine." Alton yodeled.
It all flowed together, a last dream
of lucky living and family peace,
but the brakes screamed as Alton shouted,
"Deer," and then we hit the walnut tree,
and nothing since has looked the same.

## James Lee Bucky Declines the Offer

"Ma'am," I said, speaking into the mouthpiece
of my blue cordless unit, "I don't care
if it's free or comes with fresh oysters and beer.
It's not for nothing they call it a cell phone.
It makes every place you go a jail or, worse,

an office. I've been in jail, the kind with bars
and shackles and full-time guards. The signals
let them know where you are every minute.
It's a leash, ma'am, and it will give your brain
the cancer, which I saw on 'Dateline' and believe."

Then she got quiet, so I added most likely
they knew where she was that very instant—
though I didn't—and could reel her in
if need be. "It's a fact," I said. "They control
by knowing," and that's when she asked, "Who?"

So I told her: "Aliens. I think they sent
us cell phones for surveillance, and maybe
an invasion. I don't hanker to help out,
and you be careful yourself." A silence
spoke to me across the warm morning air.

"Aliens?" she asked. "You bet, from deep space,
far beyond what we love as our galaxy.

No-sir, nothing that seems free is really free,"
which must have scared her. She hung up on me.
Now I hope I'm wrong about space invasions,

but when strangers talk to you that friendly,
you know somebody out there wants money.
And money is just where the weird shit begins.

## Leaving the Kmart 4-for-$1 Photo Portrait Booth, Junior Martin Flirts with Madness beyond the BlueLight Special and Rumors of Joy

Me, and me again, a strip of four faces
all sour and undone by work, frailed nerves,
weather, farm business, the wicked curves
of another man's woman. Disgrace is
still the natural state of natural man.
We're born into a woeful circus, cursed.
There's whiskey, dope, politics, sex, and God
to bring us to our knees. Vetch, goldenrod,
and insects from Hotlanta to Charleston
to throw a wrench into the wretched agenda.
Here's guilt's quartet of mug shots, the crime
of being me caught in four separate smirks.
That Kmart closet's just a short escape, just
light and dark four times, love and feeble lust
(whichever's what) to quarter me and send
a message to every appetite: it's time
to stop! Black swallowtails and maverick
monarchs hover and flit. Immortal ticks
dig in. The wind runs feverish, unkind
in the trees. Somebody save me from folly,
hurry, please. Somebody who won't dally.
I'm a natural man who's sinned unduly,
who loves life and daylight but truly
hates his own snide image, his dark, his mind.
Somebody punish me. Do your duty
before the evils of the heart and the flesh
and the flash in that booth drive me blind.

## Miller

High Life! Ain't that a laugh? Fool's gold
is a more right name for this bottled beer.
But listen here, what I've seen this afternoon
calls for stronger drink than Mr. Miller
ever brewed up yonder. You know I've been
an orderly at Lee County Medical for nearly
a year now. True, a disorderly orderly,
but I get my paycheck just the same.
I make enough to keep Hilda and the kids
in clothes and me half drunk insane,
but this sight I've seen will make me seem
crazy. But wait. It ain't me that's far gone.
In one of them locked lab rooms, the docs
have a freezer big enough for six sides
of prime beef. Course, there's freezers
everywhere keeping chemicals and such fresh,
but this one's full of slimy afterbirths. Yeah,
you understand me right: placentas. Yuck.
I always figured they flushed them away,
or maybe I didn't give it one think at all,
but when I swung that door open, I near
had my own hissy fit. A nurse said,
just calm as you please, "It's okay,
Pete, just placentas." "Just" my ass! So
of course, I asked, "Why?" Well-sir, no man

could guess at all the research they do
with them things and our tax money. Still,
the kicker is, some of them go to old
Procter and Gample and end up in shampool.
Think about that next time you lather up.
Hell, could be some in this here beer,
or the beer I just put away. Sure, you can
uncap me another longneck. Listen, nurse
told me once a Chinese woman asked
for hers right back, and on the spot—get
ready—she ate it. Like some mare left
to lick her foal clean in the pasture.
You're not so far from the farm you don't
remember what that looks like, and sparrows
pecking at the red remains. I saw once
an afterbirth snagged on a bob wire fence,
waving in the wind like a lost feed sack
or some kinda bloody flag. Course, by dawn
it was long gone. But a woman who wants
to swallow her own . . . I tell you, it's less
natural than that huge white icebox full
of the first suits all them babies wore. I'd
hate to think of some pervert in New York
washing his stringy hair with my Sudie's,
or some cheap politician's trollop soaking
in a tub and rubbing flesh of my flesh
into her unholy hair. We always say
that Seminoles was savage to take scalps,
but we got more than a little savage in us,
even at the hospital where you expect
everything to be neat as a milking barn.

There's something mighty sick going round,
even down to naming the poison we use
to piss our paychecks and livers away.
Have you ever thought about why some fool
might want to call this stuff "High Life"
when "Low Life" is truer and so less cruel?

## He Has Seen More Than He Bargained For

Friend, I have just attended a rattlesnake rodeo.
Down in Opp, just past Goshen and Friendship,
the Lions hold a contest to see who'll catch
the most and biggest serpent creatures wintering
down in gopher holes. Folks come from counties
and states away just to buy snakeskin wallets
and fried diamondback on a stick, spit Red Man
for distance and prizes, and eat green cotton
candy. I saw men fall from the sky and get saved
by silk, and a Chinese broke bricks with his hand.
I saw homemade sheath knives and buck dancers
gone wild as a fiddler with missing fingers sawed.
I saw Christians take up the snake and look hard
into the crude jewels of his eyes while redwings
perched on fence posts and daffodils leaned
into the speech of the wind. I saw an albino boy
hoof it like a puppet, then hand out tracts
while high school cuties in cleavage dresses
pranced on a stage, hoping to be queen. Fellows
wrestled in a pit of mud, and a tight plaid shirt
on a brown-headed gal read, "I'm proud to be
a Redneck." They milk rattlesnake fangs
for poison used in medicine. It's ugly, barrels
filled with those twisters like all of Hell's devils,
all chattering to strike some careless pilgrim.
I couldn't invent this shit, drunk or sober.

In the end, two dozen grown men stripped off
ties and shirts to chase a piglet all greased
with Crisco, while on stage, a wheelchair major
with medals leaned up to kiss the beauty
winner and crowned her with a gold circle
shaped like the meanest snake you could dream,
head raised, fangs ready, but sun-glittered.
I hopped in my truck and made tracks straight
back to tell you of the crazoids in our state.
Just bring me a fifth of Hiram Walker Green
and wipe away that creepy pit viper grin.
I'm going to loosen up now and get tight.

## Working Up a Thirst in the
## Hollow Log Lounge

It's a sign, friend, when the wells
dry up and corn dies on the stalk,
the silks brittle and shucks too dull
to cut your palm. "Dust" is the word
of the day every day around Lee County
and no church words or fancy science
can alter by an inch the way my lake's
water level drops. Fish won't bite,
'maters won't grow sweet. We're eating
beans and okra Mae put up for donation
to some worthy poor at Christmas. Listen,
even the sky itself ain't right. I've been
noticing a streak of green on the horizon
every evening. It's a portent sign
sure as bats gather in my attic to sleep
and piss and groom. I try to figure
who has done what wrong to earn this
punishment. I keep my pastures fenced,
my garden weeded. When the color peels,
I strip the board and batten back to wood
and repaint it pretty. My tools are sharp
and the engines are oiled just right. My wife
gets most of what she wants, and my tithe
hits the offering basket right on time.
A man keeps up with the Almanac, hates
meanness, and keeps his milking barn clean
enough to discourage the biting flies.

He helps a neighbor rick the hay, cuts his
meat right on the joint, and then the rain
gives up and spoils it all. I'm pondering
how I'll have to drill another hole, closer
to the lake and deeper. That's days
of work and no guarantee. The TV says
the sun's a wonder, a miracle, a star,
but I blame it just the same. I mean,
here we are, being human hard as we can,
and the only thing green on the land
is that thin blade of eerie light at dusk.
You won't make me accept in Christian
quiet a stinginess I can't understand.
What I need now is a cool shot glass
of Wild Turkey in my dry and open hand.

## March, and Mae Fields Tells
## the Most Recent Miracle She Sort of Saw

It happened. That funnel tossed mobile homes
and oaks, tore up signs, shook Hurtsboro
one hard time with a wind that come
direct from Hell, or I don't know my Bible,
though some called it the Whirling Word of God.
But when the sky got still, that weird light
green in the distance, Stella Briles
run outside looking for her son Jim
and seen his midnight Camaro smashed
under a slash pine that fell all the way
from near Spencer's Drugs.

                              I tell you, some things
don't bear up under a hard look. The mind
ain't big enough.

                    That woman bent,
her sickly and almost fifty, and she lifted
one limb no Goliath could raise. Racine
Cooper says he seen it, her face all red
in the greeny needles. Davy Roy pulled
Jimbo out, alive but broke, and that Stella heaved
her tree down and screamed for Doc Johnson,
him already busy cleaning up his own yard,
but he grabbed his bag and went like a rocket.
He took the oath, you know. Devoted.

Downtown
Deke Abbott's Homelite power saw burred bee-sy,
then quit cold, folks milling like after a funeral
and keeping eyes hawkish for the funnel.
If a pale rider comes once, he can come again.

Soon everything come about real still, dark settling
and the crickets commencing to rasp
like they was sharpening something small
and wicked, though God only knows where that brethren
rode out the blow, and Stella standing on the paving,

hands damp with blood and rosin. A man
from the paper asked her just how it felt
to have such power hold her, and she said,
"Good. I was a cloud myself, but after
was better, and I hope with all that's Holy
they can save my Jimmy's legs," as if
that was enough to explain a swarming storm
that socked in like the Devil's own doing.

I reckon that's about what you'd expect,
her being a deep-dyed Pentecostal and knowing
you don't get but one good shot, so you best
get it right, death being a thing
that strikes in the damp air, sudden.
                                    First thing
we fixed was tombstones tumped over in Green Park,
and we're walking cautious. You know, the snakes
wind will roust out, despite this chilly spell.
We're hardly heathens, you know, though a little raw,
and this clear day in scoured Lee County, we all take
our coffee strong and listen hard for the fire alarm.

We walk our mussed lawns with caution.
You know, snakes, in spite of this cold spell
the radio station says can't possibly be natural.
Neighbors say she lifted up that hunk of timber
cool as a wrestler. That Stella Briles is special.
In times like this, it's good to know she's ours.

## Goatsucker: Dillard Ramsey
## Admits to His Suspicions

They will tell you, the experts,
a bird won't do that, can't ever
fly up under a nanny
and milk her dry, but I've seen
empty udders red in the morning
and heard the nighthawks shrilling
in a honey poplar. Uncle Gizmo
Fitzgerald who lives
in the school bus down yonder
in the black raspberries
had a nanny goat
to wither up and die.
Them cicadas seen it.
That's what they're telling us,
and vampy bats will drain the blood
from a brown cow. Creatures
of the air have their own plan going.
In the country, it comes down to hunger.
It's lovely, sure, along there by the river,
but I won't go past the muscadine arbor—
even to cut new rhubarb—after the sky
edges up with evening rust,
unless there's enough ice
in the tin dipper to promise
it too cold for them goatsuckers,
them killfairies, to caper or fly.

## Jane Lagrone Rejects a Tract
## En Route to Happy Hour

Sister, the paper said some fools out west—
Kansas, I think it was—been Born
Again so hard they believe God
is fighting His way back right now.
They've all cashed in their earthly wealth—
these folks are CPA's and lawyers,
not just slow dirt farmers like my Bob—
and spend their days in a rented field
the government pays somebody to keep fallow
and hold their arms up to the sun
like reinventing prayer. They're
getting sunburned out there. Been at it
two weeks. Kids too. Ever since
a hunk of rock came down and set
the weeds afire—meteor. These people claim
it the first star to fall in what just might
be a regular hail of righteousness.
They say evil has got too huge
for churches to stop, or collections,
or the TV guy with a toupee and white socks
waving his Bible and singing his address.
There is a pain that lives in people,
Sister, that wants a reason. When I read
how folks seek out more than their share
of suffering, my heart bleeds, no matter
how much they're earth's common dunces.

Looking up and expecting, they're far
off-target and pitiful, but no worse
than you or me, I reckon. No, Sister,
I don't want your lily-white brochure
or homespun goodwill, your prayers
or reasons to be happy and follow you
walking from shadow to light, dressed up
in black to ambush anybody thirsty
and weary after a loom-room shift.
Saving your own self should be enough,
and good luck to you in these dirty times,
but pray for those pilgrims in Kansas.
I'm sure they'd like that. What my heart
needs is the Green Marguerita special,
but bless you just the same. Before the stars
come tumbling down, I mean to set
some fires of my own with Mexican tequila,
boogie sweat, and the Cherokee bartender
who rubs the goblet rim with extra salt.

## Sheriff Matt Whitlock Confesses to a Lesson in Zen after Hours

I like it quiet like this, Alton. I like
to think. I love the way spring light falls
easy, soft. This morning I was driving
the cruiser, savoring gold pollen everywhere
out in the south of the county. Real nice,
seeing forsythia and daffodils, ditch irises,
and a few Cherokee roses opening white.
It was a blue day, and I had a Tampa Jewel,
just counting cows, seeing an April breeze
in the catkins and new leaves, the radio off.
I know that's hardly right, but curse
any citizen who'd grudge me an hour's peace.
Then I started seeing this marksmanship
in the caution signs, the yellow diamonds
that warn of deer or curves ahead, a steep
grade—there's one of those. Four circles
and a jagged hole, likely a thirty-eight
slug, smack in the center neater than Willard
cleaves meat at the joint. A dozen and more.
I got mad because I get paid to protect
what the county commission declares holy—
the park with its petting zoo, the rebel
sentry on the square, and all the highway signs—
and here's all indications that some felon
has no respect, some felon who can shoot.

I admit my feelings were mixed, that right
indignation at the broken law, but envy
of his eye for centers. Mind you, I saw nary
a rip on the fringes or a near miss. Bull's-eyes,
every sign I saw. A fool is what I feel, you
understand, cause I motored over to Pig Burton's
store near The Bottle and asked him—he was
stacking feed sacks on Robert Ring's vehicle—
who the hell was the target king of Beat Three.
Pig always has his hands in every pie; he'd
know if some individual had been hauling off all
the turkey shoot prizes. I know I should know,
too, but a sheriff's got beaucoup chores
to do, mostly idiot paperwork. I've lost touch
since the last bond vote hired me four new
deputies, all dirt-dumb. Well, old Pig has
that laugh he can't hold back, and he points
his finger pistol-like at Robert, who's got
a shamed look on his face. "Pow," he says
at me or Bob, looking back and forth, just
"Pow." Seems Bob's boy Earl, the one
that ain't got the sense of a chicken under
that cowlick red as a rooster comb, is known
to have sneaked Bob's Colt a week before
and shot every yellow sign he could till his pa
ran him down and whacked him good,
then locked him in the fall-down curing shed
overnight—he's a hard man, but he loves
that boy. I remember once . . . but how the hell
can any half-wit you wouldn't trust to milk
hit the bull by the eye first time he ever gets
loose with a handgun? "It's easy," says Bob,

less shamed than afraid now he'll have to pay
for fresh metal—his people have always
been tight—but he's showing a grin I don't like.
"Real easy. He just cuts loose from the hip,
five short feet back, sometimes maybe six,
and comes back later to paint the target circles
wheresomever his bullet hits. He aims that
paintbrush right smart." Blessed if I don't
feel the fool for being full dumbstruck
at a trick Earl's not bright enough to see
as a joke. But I didn't write it up nor charge
a soul, just ground my cigar in the dirt
and helped myself to a Dr. Pepper, made believe
it didn't mean a thing, but all day I've been
riding, listening to crime reports on state radio—
robbery at the mall, attempted rape maybe, wrecks
on the bypass and a set fire in Brill's deer woods.
It gets to be too much. I shouldn't even take
the time to sit here watching this dark space
where folks have been dancing all evening,
hearing the quiet after all those raucous songs,
but Alton, don't you see, the feeble boy's right,
or half right, at least? It all comes to the same,
whether you get what you want in the end or
want what you get. The law works that way:
each law makes more crime, but it's not my job
to say. Warm up my cup just one last time.
I've got to circle Ampex once more before
I turn it home. God, this dark feels right,
no matter what flowers out there shed spring
light. The dark is what hits me as holy.
I'm calling it a day. Catch you later. Night.

## The End: Sam Buckhannon's Lament as Told to Pattie Holcey

Yeah, the Hollow Log went to disco not long
after you left to wait tables or tend Walt's seafood
buffet. I turned my back two weeks to haul a load
of canned peas to New York and came roaring back
to find a female band in satin pants and punk
hair like up north singing top forty with a fake
country slant. Del Monte peaches, particleboard
tables, treadmill machines—the stuff I tote is bad,
but back here's worse. No sign of Alton Harmon
stacking glasses or Harry with his visions of man
creatures from the sea. All my running mates
are scattered like road dust or that watery juice
that seeps out when a case of cans gets crushed
and busts. Even you, doll, spreading red crab
legs over ice. It ain't natural. Who eats that crap,
the ugly mussels and raw shrimps? Don't you miss
the little skirts y'all wore, the music and big tips,
big spenders like the fellow who swore he sold
yard animals out in Beat Four? Self-uncontrol
was our trademark. Green hats you wore on Irish
night, now that was cute. Walt's fancy sushi fish
is far from food, and this nursey white outfit
he's got you in can't do your good curves justice.
The skirt's cut's an insult to what's on my mind.
Sure, the dance floor's bigger and Sheriff Matt

never has to deal in the parking lot with knives,
but those horror movie women can't harmonize.
It's not natural. No more lonely drinkers
made welcome to perch on tall stools and cuss
the last war, weather, Revelation's fifth horse
carrying false prophets amok. Them college kids
don't give a damn to hear my gripes on speed
limits, weight limits, taxes, quota-mad troopers.
No more farmers from the Moose and their wives
come for the joy-jolt of weekend whiskey sours
and out-of-date dance steps. Stuffed critters
that lined the walls like a zoo are all missing,
and not even Walt's world-famous catfish
with pepper and raw oysters make up for the loss.
Listen, sugar, you tell Walt his sauce is still
special, but where do the textile people go
when the eagle flies, and how about Uniroyal's
cutback survivors? Spruced up and still high
on a red pill last night, I saw backup singers
in silver sequins and lace-up boots. They looked
on fire, no lie. Not even crazy Collie Chisum
could find that pink hair pretty, and bouncers
stamp a Donald Duck on your hand if you want
to step out. They charge a cover, and the fox
is gone. Who do they think they are?
I know I ought to shut up and smell out
a new second home—Rusty's, O's, the Low
Dollar Bar—but it's hard to give up Doc's
stories and happy hour that comes on whim.
I know there's a grim lesson in this. I know
to savor life's sweet meat and spit out bones.

Can't bring back what's dead or stop the will
of progress, but I miss Hank on the jukebox
as glasses clinked and cigarette smoke curled
like blue magic, the lazy fan, the lazier clock.
I miss the stuffed fox's thinning fur. The world
reflected in his glass eye could cast a spell.
Yeah, I miss his snarl.

Illinois Poetry Series
*Laurence Lieberman, Editor*

The Ways We Touch
*Miller Williams* (1997)

The Rooster Mask
*Henry Hart* (1998)

The Trouble-Making Finch
*Len Roberts* (1998)

Grazing
*Ira Sadoff* (1998)

Turn Thanks
*Lorna Goodison* (1999)

Traveling Light:
Collected and New Poems
*David Wagoner* (1999)

Some Jazz a While:
Collected Poems
*Miller Williams* (1999)

The Iron City
*John Bensko* (2000)

Songlines in Michaeltree: New and
Collected Poems
*Michael S. Harper* (2000)

Pursuit of a Wound
*Sydney Lea* (2000)

The Pebble: Old and New Poems
*Mairi MacInnes* (2000)

Chance Ransom
*Kevin Stein* (2000)

House of Poured-Out Waters
*Jane Mead* (2001)

The Silent Singer: New and Selected
Poems
*Len Roberts* (2001)

The Salt Hour
*J. P. White* (2001)

Guide to the Blue Tongue
*Virgil Suárez* (2002)

The House of Song
*David Wagoner* (2002)

X =
*Stephen Berg* (2002)

Arts of a Cold Sun
*G. E. Murray* (2003)

Barter
*Ira Sadoff* (2003)

The Hollow Log Lounge
*R. T. Smith* (2003)

## National Poetry Series

Eroding Witness
*Nathaniel Mackey* (1985)
Selected by Michael S. Harper

Palladium
*Alice Fulton* (1986)
Selected by Mark Strand

Cities in Motion
*Sylvia Moss* (1987)
Selected by Derek Walcott

The Hand of God and a Few Bright
Flowers
*William Olsen* (1988)
Selected by David Wagoner

The Great Bird of Love
*Paul Zimmer* (1989)
Selected by William Stafford

Stubborn
*Roland Flint* (1990)
Selected by Dave Smith

The Surface
*Laura Mullen* (1991)
Selected by C. K. Williams

The Dig
*Lynn Emanuel* (1992)
Selected by Gerald Stern

My Alexandria
*Mark Doty* (1993)
Selected by Philip Levine

The High Road to Taos
*Martin Edmunds* (1994)
Selected by Donald Hall

Theater of Animals
*Samn Stockwell* (1995)
Selected by Louise Glück

The Broken World
*Marcus Cafagña* (1996)
Selected by Yusef Komunyakaa

Nine Skies
*A. V. Christie* (1997)
Selected by Sandra McPherson

Lost Wax
*Heather Ramsdell* (1998)
Selected by James Tate

So Often the Pitcher Goes to Water
until It Breaks
*Rigoberto González* (1999)
Selected by Ai

Renunciation
*Corey Marks* (2000)
Selected by Philip Levine

Manderley
*Rebecca Wolff* (2001)
Selected by Robert Pinsky

Theory of Devolution
*David Groff* (2002)
Selected by Mark Doty

Rhythm and Booze
*Julie Kane* (2003)
Selected by Maxine Kumin

Other Poetry Volumes

*Local Men* and *Domains*
*James Whitehead* (1987)

Her Soul beneath the Bone:
Women's Poetry on Breast Cancer
*Edited by Leatrice Lifshitz* (1988)

Days from a Dream Almanac
*Dennis Tedlock* (1990)

Working Classics: Poems on
Industrial Life
*Edited by Peter Oresick and Nicholas
Coles* (1990)

Hummers, Knucklers, and Slow
Curves: Contemporary Baseball
Poems
*Edited by Don Johnson* (1991)

The Double Reckoning of
Christopher Columbus
*Barbara Helfgott Hyett* (1992)

Selected Poems
*Jean Garrigue* (1992)

New and Selected Poems, 1962–92
*Laurence Lieberman* (1993)

The University of Illinois Press
is a founding member of the
Association of American University Presses.

Composed in 10.5/14 Minion
with Giddyup display
by Type One, LLC
for the University of Illinois Press
Designed by Paula Newcomb
Manufactured by Cushing-Malloy, Inc.

University of Illinois Press
1325 South Oak Street
Champaign, IL 61820-6903
www.press.uillinois.edu